100

THINGS TO DO IN
BIRMINGHAM
BEFORE YOU
DIE

• •

VERNA GATES

REEDY PRESS

Library of Congress Control Number: 2017934503

ISBN: 9781681060934

Design by Jill Halpin

Cover image: Butch Oglesby, Blue Moon Studios

Printed in the United States of America
17 18 19 20 21 22   5 4 3 2 1

Please note that websites, phone numbers, addresses, and company names are subject to change or cancellation. We did our best to relay the most accurate information available, but due to circumstances beyond our control, please do not hold us liable for misinformation. When exploring new destinations, please do your homework before you go.

DEDICATION

To the city of my birth and my heart.
Your iron mountains always pull me back,
like a magnet to my soul.

CONTENTS

● ●

Music and Entertainment

● ●

• •

Culture and History

Shopping and Fashion

• •

PREFACE

It was called the Magic City—a bright, shiny new boomtown following the misery of the Civil War. Birmingham was teething on steel as a brash Wild West town with gambling, shootouts, and famous madams. When the steel died down, banking and medical industries settled it into a sophisticated city with a famed culinary scene, a broad entertainment district, and striking natural beauty. The colorful past remains in a juke joint, a haunted cemetery, and mining sites transcending into a greenway connecting the city from east to west. The city changed the country with its notorious struggle preserved in churches, parks, and the Birmingham Civil Rights Institute. The city is experiencing a new boom in the restoration of its historic downtown, craft beer scene, up and coming new chefs, and an explosion of music venues. The Magic is back.

ACKNOWLEDGMENTS

I want to thank the Alabama Tourism Department for their handy "100 Dishes to Eat Before You Die" list, and for giving me the opportunity to show off this wonderful place I call home. It is a pleasure working with the Birmingham Convention and Visitor's Bureau, who have taught me so much about my own city. Thank you, Mark Peavy, for your fabulous photos of the city we both love. Thank you to Annette Thompson for giving me such a great start on this book.

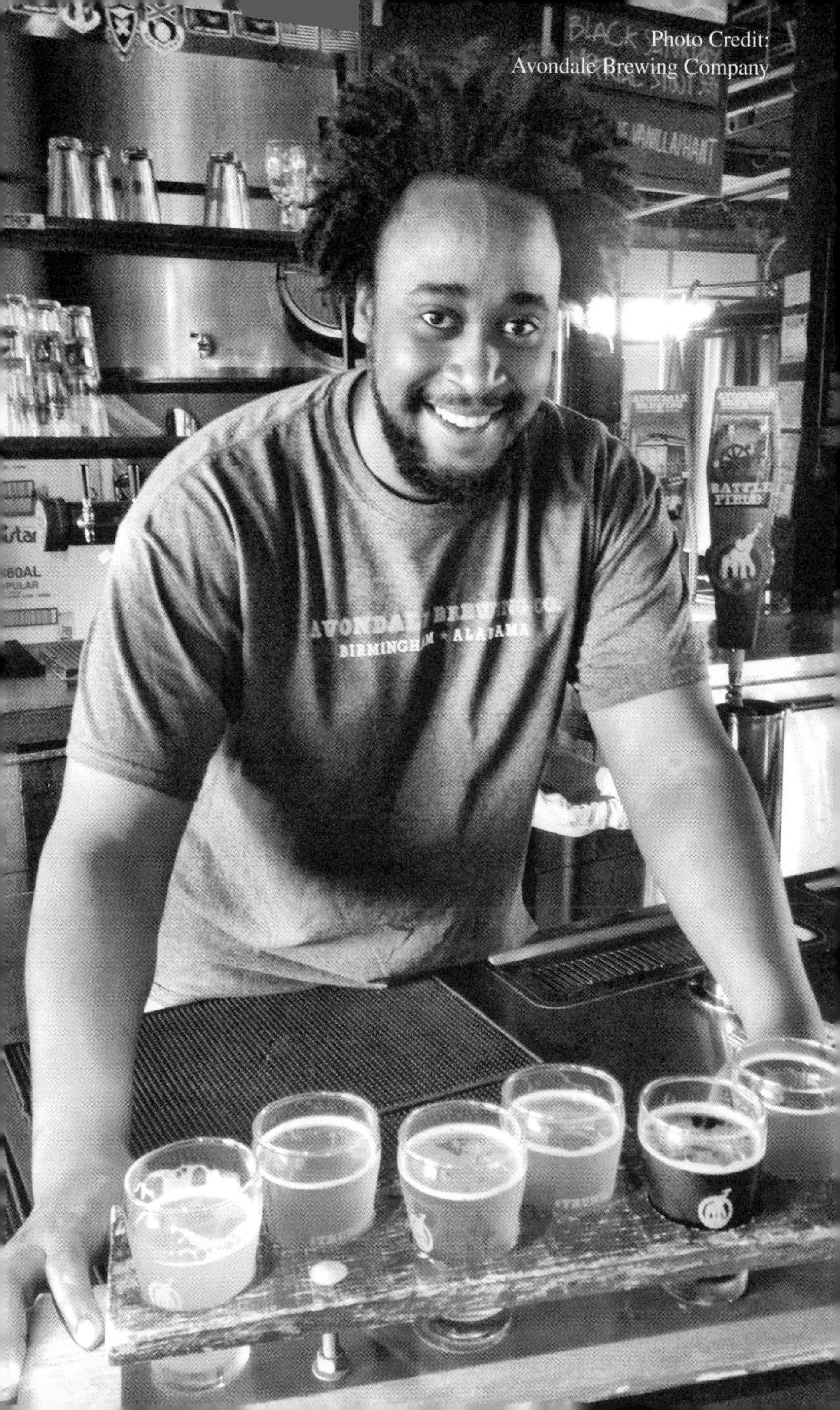

Photo Credit:
Avondale Brewing Company

FOOD AND DRINK

FRENCH TWIST ON SOUTHERN STANDARDS
AT HIGHLANDS AND CHEZ FONFON

Frank Stitt returned from training in Provence with a specific goal in mind—to put a French twist on Southern ingredients. He opened Highlands Bar & Grill in 1982, setting a new standard in the locally grown food movement. He soon opened Bottega Restaurant and Bottega Café, both inspired by Italian food. He returned to his roots with the casual French bistro, Chez Fonfon. Locals know to arrive early on Thursdays at Highlands and Fonfon to savor the crab cakes. Dishes on the 100 Things to Eat in Alabama Before You Die include baked grits at Highlands, desserts at Chez Fonfon, and parmesan soufflé at Bottega. Enjoy an "orange thing" before dinner, which is a delightfully refreshing martini creation from the bar. A frequent James Beard nominee and winner, Stitt is considered one of the best chefs in the Southeast. City leaders often gather for a drink at Highlands Bar.

2011 11th Avenue South, Birmingham
www.highlandsbarandgrill.com; www.fonfonbham.com

Bottega
2240 Highland Avenue, Birmingham
www.bottegarestaurant.com

ONE OF THE HOTTEST RESTAURANTS,
HOT AND HOT FISH CLUB

When tomatoes come into season, the word goes out for the beloved Hot and Hot Tomato Salad listed on the *100 Dishes to Eat in Alabama Before You Die,* along with the Pickled Okra. Chef and owner of Hot and Hot Fish Club and Ovenbird, Chris Hastings has captured James Beard awards and also defeated Bobby Flay in Iron Chef America, with a dish now served as his Iron Chef Ravioli. Hot and Hot blends French, California, and Southern cooking styles plus local farmers' produce into a unique flavor. Ovenbird opens into the Garden of Charlie and Cindy Thigpen, with its open door and open fire concept restaurant. The small plate menu offers delicacies, ranging from a Beef Fat Candle to Octopus Salad. The live fire grilling theme originated in Spanish and Southern traditions. A local beer company created a signature brew for Ovenbird to complement its craft cocktails.

2180 11th Court South,
Birmingham,
205-933-5474
www.hotandhotfishclub.com

2810 3rd Avenue South,
Birmingham,
205-957-6686
www.ovenbirdrestaurant.com

LET THE GOOD TIMES ROLL
AT CAFÉ DUPONT

Chris Dupont's New Orleans roots shine through in the polished woods and exposed bricks of its circa 1870 historic downtown building. Designed as a traditional bistro, the soft lighting and vintage touches spark romance. The food, which changes daily, comes together with the same perfect touch of old and new. The buttermilk on your buttermilk fried chicken with lemon beurre blanc sauce probably came from the nearby Wright Dairy, where the family milks, bottles, and sells right on the farm. Or smear a classic beignet with homemade strawberry preserves. Signature dishes include fried oysters & okra with cayenne butter sauce, seared sea scallops with goat cheese souffle, and grilled dry-aged beef ribeye. On Wednesday night, the Sidebar hosts happy hour from 5:00 p.m. to 7:00 p.m.

113 20th Street North, Birmingham, 205-322-1282
www.cafedupont.net

PEDDLE INTO
THE WOODLAWN CYCLE CAFÉ

Deceptively simple, the Woodlawn Cycle Café sits behind an unassuming white façade. Inside, plain wooden tables include a farm table where you can sit with friends you just met. A short list of options line the menu. Your five choices could include a mushroom sandwich, empanadas with braised oxtail with crème fraiche, or pork stew. Hipster in a throwback kind of way, there is no Wi-Fi, no social media, and no phone in case it might disturb the conversation. The café focuses on doing a few things exquisitely well. Open for breakfast, the espresso blends with homemade honey-nut granola, a toastie with salad, or a sweet potato biscuit crowned with pepper jelly. In the evening, pasta has been perfected.

5530 1st Avenue South, Birmingham, 205-867-5309

FORAGING FOR THE BEST BISCUITS
AT FEAST AND FOREST

Arrive early on a Saturday morning to get a seat before the brunch crowd, or you will have to take out your avocado toast with a scrambled egg, chive cream cheese, and marinated peppers. Be careful with the buttermilk biscuit that is so light that it might just float off the plate. Smear some house jams over it, preferably the orange marmalade. For lunch, the roasted beet bowl can make you crave vegetables. No worries. The sweets from Bandit Baking Company can bring you back from too many healthy thoughts. When they bring out the warm, just-baked rosemary shortbread, the scent alone will alert your mouthwatering response. Try one and top it off with a rich, melt-in-your-mouth brownie and a cappuccino.

212 24th Street North, Birmingham, 205-920-1862
www.feastandforest.com

CIRCLE THE GLOBE
AT PIZITZ FOOD HALL

The elegant old downtown Pizitz department store stands for fashion once again. The Pizitz Food Hall is packing in patrons for lunch, dinner, and drinks. Breakfast begins with Revelator Coffee, Waffle Works, and Alabama Biscuit Co. Try Asian for lunch with a ramen noodle stand: Ichicoro Imoto, mo:mo: for Asian noodles; and Ono Poke for a Japanese/Hawaiian fusion. Tacos and burritos contribute Mexican flare. For that afternoon snack, the Busy Corner Cheese & Provisions sell artisanal cheeses and an original twist on the classic grilled cheese sandwich. For dinner, choose from Ethiopian (Ghion Cultural Hall), Israeli (Eli's Jerusalem Grill), Italian (Fero), or American (the Standard, Reveal Kitchen). Dessert cools the palate with Lichita's ice cream and Mexican paletas. Indulge in a craft cocktail at the Louis, a bar named for the original owner, Louis Pizitz.

120 19th Street North, Birmingham, 205-639-0108
www.thepizitz.com/food-hall

RED LIGHT MEANS GO
TO CHEZ LULU

With rich, warm red walls, crushed velvet pillows, and velvet paintings, Chez Lulu makes a tongue-in-cheek reference to French "Madame Lulu's"—code for red light districts. Add sidewalk seating and Chez Lulu captures the best of French café society. The food, featuring soups, tarts, pizza, and a long list of delectable desserts, is inspired by the authentic European breads baked in the adjoining Continental Bakery, which is where the café idea began. Some come to Lulu just for the Lulu cheese with fresh bread or the salad sampler. While the restaurant may teasingly recall a bordello, the bakery operates as a serious medieval shop, with Old World handcrafted skill and natural ingredients going into every baguette. The art of food is occasionally accompanied by an accordian, dancers, opera singers, jugglers, Brazilian drum corps, or Moroccan gypsy fiddlers.

1911 Cahaba Road, Birmingham, 205-870-7011
www.chezlulu.us

YOU WILL WANT TO STAY AWAKE
FOR DREAMCAKES

Children may run for the ice cream truck, but for adults, it is the Dreamcakes Cupcake Truck that inspires a dash with cash in hand, seeking your favorite flavors. The truck appears for special events or just travels around town, seeking sweet tooths. Celebrations begin with an order from Dreamcakes—weddings, anniversaries, birthdays, football victories, and other events. When you order a cake, the layers slice like a cloud of dreams, so tender is the cake. Beware of the chocolate high, one of the most popular cupcake flavors among the more than a hundred choices. The over the moon, simply strawberry, and red velvet stay in high demand. Creative custom cakes charm as well as satisfy. If a cake is too big, select macaroons, cookies, brownies, or a cannoli. Cake decorating lessons are available. Bring a friend and your favorite libation.

960 Oxmoor Road, Homewood, 205-871-9377
www.dreamcakes-bakery.com

FRESH AS AN ALPINE FOREST
AT KLINGLER'S

The Black Forest torte takes you back to an alpine vision of a quaint German village with authenticity and genuine tastiness. Listed on the 100 Dishes to Eat in Alabama Before You Die, this bakery item harkens back to the origins of Klingler's European Bakery and Café. The demand for imported deli sausages and German cuisine soon propelled the shop into a full-service breakfast/lunch restaurant. Build a brat your way with purple cabbage or sauerkraut, or choose braten beef in a pot pie. The lentil and smoked sausage soup will make you yearn for a cold winter day when it warms the palate and the body. Try the schnitzel or blintzes for breakfast.

621 Montgomery Highway, Vestavia Hills, 205-823-4560
www.klinglers.com

A VEGETARIAN'S DREAM
AT A STEAK AND SEAFOOD
RESTAURANT

More than seventy items line the long steam table at Niki's West Steak and Seafood Restaurant. The line moves fast, so try to decide early! The cafeteria line is stocked with classic Southern "meat and three" meat, and three vegetables, with a nod to the owners' Greek heritage. Good news for vegetarians is that all their veggies are cooked without traditional pork or chicken stock. Their vegetables are listed in One Hundred Dishes to Eat in Alabama Before You Die. Three menus offer a table service option, from classic breakfast to a seafood and steak menu. From the "famous" stuffed grouper to Greek-style shellfish and fish, the seafood menu items taste as fresh as the water they were swimming in that morning. Come prepared for generous portions and homemade desserts.

233 Finley Avenue, Birmingham, 205-252-8163
www.nikiswest.com

A TASTE OF THE GULF
AT THE FISH MARKET

George Sarris barely set a toe in his new American home before he found a kitchen. Arriving from Greece in 1969, he joined the Greek restaurant dynasty by washing dishes the next day at Niki's, owned by his uncles. He opened a fish market to sell Gulf shrimp and seafood, which soon morphed into the Fish Market Restaurant and Oyster House, which puts a Greek twist on Alabama fish. His famed Athenian-style fish comes topped with grilled onions, marinated Greek olives, sliced tomatoes, creamy feta cheese, and Greek spices. George's special oyster stew features plump oysters in a rich base so filling it is best eaten as an entrée. Whether Greek style or low-country po'boy, everything comes with Southern-style sides: collards, black-eyed peas and fried okra.

612 22nd Street South, 205-322-3330
www.thefishmarket.net

THE REAL
WHISTLE STOP CAFÉ

Fannie Flagg grew up eating at her great aunt's restaurant, where fried green tomatoes were a popular item at the "stand" right in front of the small-town whistle-stop. Miss Bess Fortenberry, a single lady with a zest for life, recruited two other lady friends from her work during World War II to join her in the small, but popular, Irondale Cafe. Thus began the Fried Green Tomatoes at the Whistle Stop Café of book and movie fame. The original still serves six hundred to eight hundred of the crispy fried delicacies every day. Green tomatoes are firmer than their riper cousins and thrive in hot oil, which seals their plump, fleshy texture and rich flavor. Bess' original recipe remains intact, and the café offers prepackaged boxes with the proper spices for cooking them.

1906 1st Avenue North, Irondale, 205-956-5258
www.irondalecafe.com

TIP
Come back for the Whistle Stop Festival in late September. Be sure to listen for the train riding past the café and the craft and food vendors.

STEAKS THAT HANG OFF THE PLATE
AT LLOYD'S RESTAURANT

For decades, Lloyd's Restaurant denoted the end of civilization, as far as Birmingham travelers were concerned. It stood as a lonely beacon on old Highway 280 as the last stop before the forest took over. Today, development surrounds Lloyd's, one of the oldest restaurants in town. New shops may crowd the down-home restaurant, but they can't cover the sumptuous scent of onion rings emanating from every corner since 1937. Pair those rings with a hamburger steak and you will be eating the meal that draws regulars back for more. The steaks are so big, they hang off the plate, especially the twenty ounce Porterhouse. The full menu includes seafood and barbecue, and the onion rings are listed on the 100 Dishes to Eat in Alabama Before You Die.

5301 U.S. 280, Hoover, 205-991-5530
www.lloyds280.com

SOUL FOOD
FROM THE HEART
AT EAGLE'S RESTAURANT

Soul food originated from parts considered unsuitable for fancy tastes, but African-American cooks turned pig's ears into the silk purses of flavor. Andrew Zimmern of the Food Network noted the visible bristles along the ear's rim as a sign of genuine soul food in Birmingham's premier soul food spot, Eagle's Restaurant. The family cooks the fatty pig's feet, eking out every nuance of tastiness. For the pork neck bones, they cut and wash each one by hand, slow cooked until it melts into its own gravy. The two most expensive menu items come from the humblest ingredients: the chitterlings (intestines) and the ox tail. Please do not attempt cutlery on the tender tail, their most famous dish, or you are in danger of being branded a Yankee. It is properly devoured using the fingers.

2610 16th Street North, Birmingham, 205-320-0099
www.eaglesrestaurant.com

CODDLE YOUR EGG
AT SATTERFIELD'S

As a stay-at-home mom, Becky Satterfield grew organic vegetables and watched Julia Child, never suspecting the two would one day merge into one of Birmingham's best restaurants. Satterfield's Restaurant "grew organically," much like the meat and produce she so carefully selects for her often French-based recipes. Her popular Coddled Egg appetizer is classic Satterfield: caramelized onion, carrots, and celery doused with cream and cheese, with the pierced yolk of a poached egg—comfort food supreme. Take a Southern standard, such as pork chops and a sweet potato, add a bacon-stuffed chili relleno on a bed of apple molé, and the result is the highly recommended Duroc Pork Chop. Top it off with beignets with sauteed apples and homemade vanilla bean ice cream.

3161 Cahaba Heights Road, Vestavia Hills, 205-969-9690
satterfieldsrestaurant.com

YOU'LL BE OVER THE MOON
AT THE BRIGHT STAR

An itinerant artist needed a few good meals as he traveled through the South. The long-forgotten artist left behind classical murals in the restaurant that has surpassed its 100th birthday. The Bright Star began as a horseshoe-shaped café bar founded by a Greek immigrant. Today, it seats 330 and is operated by two brothers, descendants of early owners. In 2010, the James Beard Foundation named it an American Classic, a lifetime achievement. What hasn't changed is the Greek-style snapper and steaks, the fried snapper throats, and the homemade seafood gumbo. The 100 Dishes to Eat in Alabama Before You Die list's broiled seafood platter is a fish lover's dream with Gulf red snapper, shrimp, oysters, and scallops, finished off with lobster and crab meat au gratin. The homemade pies tower with whipped meringue. At lunch, you can indulge in a meat-and-three menu.

304 19th Street North, Bessemer, 205-426-1861
www.thebrightstar.com

A FAMILY AFFAIR
AT GIANMARCO'S

In the beginning, Birmingham attracted large numbers of Italian immigrants, setting a high bar for great Italian food. Gianmarco's Restaurant raised that bar. Owned by an Italian father and two sons, the family pride in cuisine breaks out into fettuccini, linguini, rigatoni, and lasagna, always served hot. The waiters line up at the open kitchen, waiting for the steaming plates to spend just moments on the counter. One of the sons, Marco, prefers old-world comfort food. When regulars get a whiff of Marco making his braciole, the non-reservation tables at the bar fill up fast. Brother Giani prefers modern fusion for creative nightly specials. Father Giovanni, the "pretty face" out front, greets guests with his charming Italian accent. The whole family turns out to hand-make the pasta from custom Italian pasta flour.

721 Broadway Steet, Homewood, 205-871-9622
www.gianmarcosbhm.com

COMFORT FOOD FOUND A NEW COMFORT ZONE
AT JOHNNY'S RESTAURANT

While you expect to see white tablecloth restaurants in the "Oscars of Food," the James Beard awards, it is rare for an old-school meat-and-three chef to get a nomination. Tim Hontzas, a member of one of Birmingham's restaurant dynasties, refers to his food as a meat-and-Greek. Along with crispy fried chicken and the greens duo collards and turnip, you will find charbroiled chicken souvlaki or keftedes (Greek meatballs). On his blackboard, he lists the menu and gives credit to his epicurean heroes—the local farmers who treat their animals with respect and their veggies with nothing at all. He insists that farmers hand-grade the picked okra heading for his frying pan. Hontzas delights in cooking up happiness or, as the blackboard suggests, make cornbread, not war.

2902 18th Street South, Suite 200, Homewood, 205-802-2711
www.johnnyshomewood.com

NEIGHBORHOOD CAFÉ WITH A MEDITERRANEAN TWIST
AT NABEEL'S CAFÉ AND MARKET

Memories of hometowns in Patras in Southern Greece and Trieste in Northern Italy led John and Ottacia Krontiras to design Nabeel's Cafe and Market around a neighborhood concept. Located in the heart of Homewood, families can walk to the shop and sit outside or slide into a booth for genuine Greek and Italian food. The Market sells hard-to-find Mediterranean foods and spices, such as olives, sheep feta, Russian sausages, dried figs, and Greek olive oils. The spanakopita (spinach pie) is baked in flaky phyllo and filled with rich feta cheese. The camel rider, selected as one of Alabama's 100 Dishes, combines beef, bologna, and salami, with provolone cheese to make a hearty sandwich. The moussaka joins the list also, with eggplant and ground beef combined into a casserole, garnished with a dollop of tomato fondue.

1706 Oxmoor Road, Homewood, 205-879-9292
www.nabeels.com

A WHOLE LOT
OF SHAKING GOING ON
AT GREEN VALLEY DRUGS

Take your seat at the historic lunch counter, or slide into a booth at Green Valley Drugs. For more than sixty years, hamburgers have sizzled on the grill along with crisp bacon for an added crunch. Or slather pimento cheese on top of the burger for the recommended medicine for hunger. The old-fashioned milk shakes stick to the basics: vanilla, chocolate, strawberry, and cherry. A homespun shake cannot be mastered with a straw; a spoon is required. The menu offers chili two ways: either canned or homemade; you can expect this level of honesty from the menu and the staff, adding even more character to the experience. Breakfast follows tradition with eggs, grits, bacon, and toast. For the biggest dose of nostalgia, check out the throwback prices.

1915 Hoover Court, Hoover, 205-822-1151

GUS, SNEAKY PETE,
AND HOT DIGGITY DOGS

Gus Alexander opened Gus's Hot Dogs in the late 1940s. He deposited the tiny shop with the big sauce in the care of Greek cousins when he decided to return home. The grilled dog, with mustard, onions, and the requisite secret sauce, was named one of America's seventy-five best by the Daily Meal. Not far away, Pete Graphos stirred up his own secret sauce and launched Sneaky Pete's Hot Dogs. His recipe mixes a beef-pork combo and contributes kraut and/or chili, bacon, and either cheese or beef sauce. Newcomer Hot Diggity Dogs skips the special sauce but does offer a choice of kosher beef or tofu. These dogs come in everything from the Diablo Dog (hot) to the Waimea Dog (spam and pineapple) to the Winky Dink Dog (pimento cheese).

Gus's Hot Dogs
1915 4th Avenue North, Birmingham, 205-251-4540

Sneaky Pete's Hot Dogs
Various locations
www.sneakypeteshotdogs.com

Hot Diggity Dogs
430 41st Street South, Suite B (upstairs), Birmingham, 205-202-2363
www.hotdiggitydogsbham.com

NAMED FOR ITS HAMBURGER,
FAMOUS FOR ITS TEA

Many people have tried to guess the secret ingredient in the famed Milo's Sweet Tea, but makers insist that the treasured elixir contains only tea and sugar. The recipe for this local favorite remains elusive to devotees who seek the original energy drink. Equally secret since its 1946 founding is the sauce generously poured over a grilled hamburger patty, smothering onions and pickles. A fresh, warm bun tops the Milo's Original Burger. For breakfast, the mini-cinnamon buns hide behind their own discreet recipe. Both the burger and tea are listed in the 100 Dishes to Eat in Alabama Before You Die. You can only get the burger at one of the many Milo's locations, but the sweet tea can be found in most food and convenience stores.

Several locations,
www.miloshamburgers.com

BLACK-EYED PEAS AND TURNIP GREENS
MAKE PIZZA SOUTHERN STYLE

Pepperoni may be the soul food of Italy, but Slice cuts a Southern path with the soul pie: Conecuh sausage, black-eyed peas, turnip greens, bacon, onions, and cheese on a razor-thin crust. With a nod to the nearby Gulf, there's an oyster Rockefeller as well. Wash it back with a cold local beer from their extensive bar. Post Office Pies made Thrilllist's Top 33 Pizza Shops in America for its swine pie, a cardiac-risking delicious lode of pepperoni, sausage, bacon, cheese, and a bit of basil. Davenport's Pizza Palace cracked the pizza market in the meat-and-three town in 1964 by hand-delivering pizzas to neighbors to introduce "foreign food." The crust is thin and comes cut into squares with your choice of toppings. Chicago-style pizza fans choose Tortugas Homemade Pizza. The deep-dish stuffed pizza is on the 100 Dishes to Eat in Alabama Before You Die list.

Slice Pizza & Brew
725 29th Street South, Birmingham, 205-715-9300
www.slicebirmingham.com

Post Office Pies
209 41st Street South, Birmingham, 205-599-9900
www.postofficepies.com

Davenport's Pizza Palace
2837 Cahaba Road, Mountain Brook, 205-879-8603
www.davenportspizza.com

Tortugas Homemade Pizza
Highway 150, Hoover, 205-403-9800
www.tortugaspizza.com

PIT MASTERS RULE
IN ALABAMA BARBECUE

The Year of Alabama Barbecue celebrated the rich tradition of the pit master. Several noted devotees of the pit fire are smoking pork throughout the Birmingham area. Jim 'n Nick's Bar-B-Q Restaurant cooks up their own heritage pigs, grown by Alabama farmers. The cheese biscuits hit the spot and the 100 Dishes list. Full Moon Bar-B-Que is famous for half-moon cookies and marinated coleslaw; both made the 100 Dishes list. The Golden Rule Bar-B-Q and Grill started as a roadhouse in 1891, making it the oldest continuously running restaurant in Alabama. Demetri's BBQ hides its barbecue in a breakfast omelet, a manly meal earning it the number one spot in Playboy's Best Breakfast in America listing. The pork-stuffed tater may be on the 100 Dishes list for highly awarded Saw's BBQ, but the pork and greens say soul food delicious. Go to the original Saw's in Avondale. You know a state takes its barbecue seriously when white sauce is considered controversial. Miss Myra has ignored the naysayers for years while diners line up to eat her crispy and moist chicken dipped in her pale sauce. Bob Sykes Bar-B-Q of Bessemer has dished up its 100 Dishes pork sandwich since 1957. Catch the ribs at Rib-It-Up downtown.

Full Moon Bar-B-Que—Several locations
www.fullmoonbbq.com

Saw's BBQ
215 41st Street South, Birmingham,
205-591-1409
www.sawsbbq.com

Golden Rule Bar-B-Q and Grill—several locations
www.goldenrulebbq.com

Bob Sykes Bar-B-Q
1724 9th Avenue North, Bessemer,
205-426-1400
www.bobsykes.com

Demetri's BBQ
1901 28th Avenue South, Homewood,
205-871-1581
www.demetrisbbq.com

Miss Myra's Pit Bar-B-Q
278 Cahaba Heights Road, Vestavia Hills,
205-967-6004

Rib-It-Up
830 1st Avenue North, Birmingham,
205-328-7427
www.Ribitup.com

BARBEQUE IN A GAS STATION?
BUTTS-TO-GO FOR THOSE ON THE GO

For twenty-one years, Wade Reich worked in the food industry in Paris and London. When he retired, he came home to Alabama and opened a Texaco station on the road to Logan Martin Lake. When gas prices rose past profitability, Wade broke out the smoker in the back of the gas station and was soon selling more Boston butts than petroleum. Butts-to-Go was born. He added a drunken chicken, potato salad made with cream cheese, Southern veggies, and lemon chicken wings that make you want to take flight. A couple of tables sit inside the station for dining, but most people choose to take out—so many, in fact, that on Talladega race days and summer weekends, Wade's food causes a traffic jam. Don't forget to gas up before you leave.

410 Martin Street, Pell City, 205-884-2888
www.buttstogo.com

POP GOES THE SUMMER HEAT
WITH POPSICLES

The giant pink popsicle and popsicle stick benches outside say it all for Sweet Bebe's Ice Cream Pops in Argo. While it advertises the watermelon flavor, the chocolate-dipped peanut butter could compete as a cold version of a popular peanut butter cup. For the adventurous, try the cantaloupe and chocolate-dipped coconut. Steel City Pops appear at gatherings with their cart, pulling out their buttermilk popsicle, which combines a complex duo of flavors: vanilla and cheesecake. Strawberry lemonade wins the popularity contest. Try the maple bacon with bourbon, the cucumber lime, or sweet tea. Urban Pops put out the regulars, but add Asian and Indian flavors to their sticks. These treats incorporate ingredients from roses to saffron to cardamom. Kulfi deepens the flavor into a richer, creamier ice cream.

Sweet Bebe's Ice Cream
1919 U.S. Highway 11, Argo, 205-572-5852
www.sweetbebes.net

Steel City Pops
2821 Central Avenue, Suite 109, Homewood, 205-803-6502
www. steelcitypops.com

Urban Pops
2760 John Hawkins Parkway, Suite 100, Hoover, 205-518-0270

WAKE-UP CALL
AT COFFEE SHOPS

Sitting on the brim of the university campus, Lucy's Coffee and Tea brags on its international clientele, who come in for coffee, sandwiches, and stellar conversation. Try the coffee smoothie for a semi-healthy caffeine rush with an egg Maclucy. Naked Art stimulates the visual senses by placing great paintings on the walls. Red Cat keeps Pepper Place and Railroad Park in stimulating drinks by providing "coffee with a conscious." They layer out the spanakopita the old, painstaking Greek way. For a true neighborhood coffee shop, Crestwood Coffee caters to its hip, artsy 'hood. Don't worry if you don't live here. You will soon feel like you do in this friendly, intimate shop. The Cuban sandwich goes best with something from the bar. Monthly art shows and used books line the walls, inviting you to stay awhile.

Lucy's Coffee & Tea
2007 University Blvd., Birmingham,
205-328-2007
www.lucyscoffeeandtea.com

Red Cat Coffee House
Pepper Place and Railroad Park, Birmingham
www.theredcatcoffeehouse.com

Crestwood Coffee
5512 Crestwood Boulevard, Birmingham,
205-595-0300

Photo Credit:
Mark Peavy

SPORTS AND RECREATION

ACCELERATE TO
TALLADEGA SUPERSPEEDWAY

The biggest, fastest, and hardest-to-win racetrack rockets at top speed at the legendary Talladega Superspeedway. To sound like a true fan, call it 'Dega. Thousands of people camp in the infield for the social event of the year—that doubles as NASCAR's greatest sporting event. Careers have been made and broken at 'Dega as they tempt the treacherous turns and heavy competition. So many people come in through the Talledega airport, it becomes the nation's busiest one weekend a year. Stroll through the infield throng of people, barbeque grills, parties, reunions, and entertainers—people watching can almost surpass keeping your eyes on the race. While there, take a track tour and visit the International Motorsports Hall of Fame, where rare car displays and driver tributes celebrate the sport. Opt for a driving experience of your own.

3366 Speedway Boulevard, Lincoln, 855-518-7223
www.talladegasuperspeedway.com

TIP

While in the area, visit the town of Talladega. It is a beautiful Victorian town that is home to the Alabama School for Deaf and Blind. Talledaga is one of the most accessible towns in America, with talking stop lights, public phone booths for the deaf, and even people who deliver pizzas have to know sign language.

Photo Credit:
Mark Peavy

GET YOUR MOTOR RUNNING
AT BARBER MOTORSPORTS

Yes, a replica of the lost Captain America bike from *Easy Rider* throttles down here. One man's passion drove him to become the world's largest collector of motorcycles. The Barber Motorsports Museum displays more than fifteen hundred motorcycles stretching across one hundred years of the two-wheeled wonders. In the historic section, early attempts at motorcycles, such as adapting bikes and even carriages, detail the beginnings of the crotch rockets seen on the level above. Rare cars and race cars line the first two floors. Designed in an ever rising circle, the gleaming machines stun with their beauty and design. The museum sits beside an active motor track where cars and motorcycles race to victory throughout the year. Adjoining the track, the Porsche Driving Experience puts you in the driver's seat.

6040 Barber Motorsports Parkway, Leeds, 205-298-9040
www.barberracingevents.com

TEE OFF
AT ROBERT TRENT JONES GOLF COURSES

Dr. David Bronner, the visionary leader of the Alabama Retirement Systems of Alabama, set out to create local tourist attractions. He partnered with famed golf course designer Robert Trent Jones to design a trail from the mountains to the beaches. The Ross Bridge course is woven into the rolling hills of Shannon Valley, creating one of the longest courses in the world. Styled in the manner of an old parkland course, ten holes border two lush lakes. The quiet waters are deceptive—they connect with a magnificent eighty-foot drop waterfall. Generous greens lure golfers to try their skills on approach shots. The adjoining resort offers plenty of bragging space on a successful game, with restaurants, bars, and a complete pro shop—and a spa for those missed swings.

4000 Grand Avenue, Hoover, 205-949-3085
www.rtjgolf.com/rossbridge/

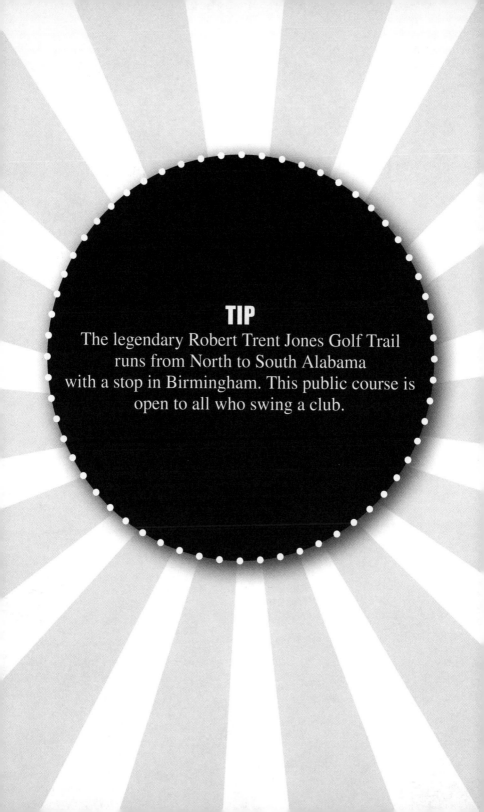

TIP

The legendary Robert Trent Jones Golf Trail
runs from North to South Alabama
with a stop in Birmingham. This public course is
open to all who swing a club.

PLAY BALL AT REGIONS FIELD/CLASSIC
AT RICKWOOD

Taking a seat in Rickwood Field, you can almost hear the crack of Babe Ruth's bat as he knocks a home run over the right field stands. Satchel Paige and Dizzy Dean threw pitches, and Willie Mays ran for first base, along with 107 other Hall of Famers who played here. Now the oldest ballpark in America, Rickwood still hosts local college and high school games. It celebrates its history annually at the Rickwood Classic, where players and audience dress in period costumes for an afternoon of nostalgia. In 2013, the Birmingham Barons moved downtown into Regions Field. The new ballpark features a view of the downtown skyline and a 360° concourse while keeping the intimate feel of the old Rickwood.

1137 2nd Avenue West, Birmingham, 205-458-8161
www.rickwood.com

1401 1st Avenue South, Birmingham, 205-988-3200
www.milb.com

HONOR THE GREATS
AT THE NEGRO SOUTHERN LEAGUES MUSEUM

When baseball became America's pastime, it caught Birmingham's passion. Leagues popped up everywhere: industrial leagues, church leagues, women's leagues, and minor league teams for white and black players. Seemingly everyone who could hold a bat played ball. This intense focus on the sport created a pipeline from Birmingham to the Negro American League and Negro National League. Famed players, such as Leroy "Satchel" Paige and Willie Mays, played for the legendary Black Barons. The Negro Southern League Museum contains the largest collection of original Negro League artifacts. A salute to Alabama's own Bo Jackson applauds the man who played major league baseball and football. Top researchers work with the museum to enhance the collection and promote understanding of the role the leagues played in transcending barriers.

120 16th Street South, Birmingham, 205-581-3040
www.birminghamnslm.org

FOOTBALL, FOOD, AND FUN
AT THE MAGIC CITY CLASSIC

Alabama and Auburn may have the biggest rivalry in the nation, but in Alabama, A&M University and Alabama State University rival their rivalry as the two largest historically black universities (HBUC) clash. Their long-running annual face-off has grown into the highest attendance of an HBUC game and the country's biggest predominately African-American event. More than two hundred thousand people join the fun at the Magic City Classic at Legion Field. While sixty thousand people crowd the stands, even more are barbecuing and tailgating in one of the biggest reunion parties in football. Everybody wins during the week of festivities. The battle of the bands pits ASU's Mighty Marching Hornets against AAMU's Maroon and White Marching Band in a triumphant on-field musical extravaganza. A parade, pep rally, block parties, and comedy show add to the high spirits of the event.

400 Graymont Avenue West, Birmingham, 205-254-2391
www.magiccityclassic.com

CANOE
THE CAHABA

A river runs through it. Birmingham is bordered by one of the last free-flowing rivers in Alabama, the Cahaba. In spite of urban sprawl, this feisty little river persists in being one of the most biodiverse rivers in the United States. Home to a whopping 131 species of fish, the Cahaba is home to more species of fish than is found in all of California. It is possible to get in the water below a highway bridge and feel as though you are in the wilderness after just a few paddle strokes. The most popular time to go is in May, when the rare and beautiful Cahaba Lily blooms in the shoals of the river. Big and white, they put on a spectacular show. Helena and Bibb County are popular put-in spots.

Canoe the Cahaba
2370 Highway 52, Helena, 205-874-5623

A ROARING GOOD TIME
AT THE BIRMINGHAM ZOO

Elephants have trumpeted throughout Birmingham's history! First, Miss Fancy carried children through Avondale Park. Then Mona arrived at the zoo in 1955. Today, the Birmingham Zoo honors their pachyderm past with national leadership in elephant conservation. The Trails of Africa blends species with a bachelor elephant herd, red river hogs, rhinos, and more. These animals are part of the 950 animals living at the zoo, representing 230 species. The exhibits include primates, big cats, sea lions, birds, amphibians, reptiles, and insects. Several of the animals, such as rhinos, are endangered. Don't miss the pirate train ride on the Birmingham Zoo Express. Animal lovers can schedule behind-the-scenes tours and personalized encounters with sea lions and the Cassowary.

2630 Cahaba Road, Birmingham, 205-879-0409
www.birminghamzoo.com

SET YOUR COMPASS
FOR OAK MOUNTAIN STATE PARK

The hiking, camping, fishing, swimming, and canoeing bring throngs of people to Oak Mountain State Park. A golf course, horse barn, trails, and a BMX track combine to appeal to those who like both slow and speedy sports. However, the mountain biking and orienteering make Oak Mountain famous. The Double Oak Trail, built by mountain bikers, is one of fifty-two places worldwide listed as an Epic Ride. The twenty-six mile train climbs nineteen hundred feet with tight singletrack and five miles of loop doubletrack. With two mountain ridges and diverse landscapes, Oak Mountain ranks among the best places to go orienteering. A competitive sport, orienteering is essentially a race using a map and a compass. Afterward, spread out a picnic on one of the many tables or under shady trees.

200 Terrace Drive, Pelham, 205-620-2524
www.alapark.com/oak-mountain-state-park
www.vulcanorienteering.org

GET ROLLING
AT RAILROAD PARK

Pass by what was once a decrepit railroad dump and see people walking, tossing Frisbees, picnicking, and relaxing. Once an eyesore, Railroad Park transcended into a stunning, award-winning public park. This new oasis looks out onto the city skyline through a lake, six hundred trees, and nine acres of lawn. Far from a barren grassland, native plants dot the pathways, and a wetland attracts noisy, colorful birds. Memories of the old site remain in benches made from repurposed materials, and hand-made bricks and cobblestones placed throughout. Come here for a stroll, for the playground, to hear a band, or for a movie night. What you will see are families and friends enjoying a park that doubles as a catalyst for Birmingham's downtown renaissance.

1600 1st Avenue South, Birmingham, 205-521-9933
www.railroadpark.org

AVONDALE PARK
SAVED THE CITY

Miss Fancy, an elephant, once dominated Avondale Park, where the original zoo was housed. This historic park saved Birmingham's founding fathers when they discovered the underground springs provided the only clean water during a cholera epidemic that threatened to pull the curtain on the Magic City. It is the site of Birmingham's only Civil War skirmish in 1865, when a few Union soldiers stopped to water their horses and were met by a local guard. Only the lady who owned the property received a bullet wound. Today, the spring feeds a duck pond, the fields display art shows, and the amphitheater hosts jazz concerts and theater performances. Instead of riding high on Miss Fancy's back, today's children play in the ball fields and tennis courts. Marriages, reunions, and special events are celebrated in the restored villa.

4101 5th Avenue South, Birmingham, 205-254-2556
www.birminghamal.gov/parks-and-recreation

TIP
Walk across the street for a hotdog at Hot Diggity Dog. Eat it while watching the ducks swim in the pond.

SNOWFLAKES
IN ALDRIDGE GARDENS

Hydrangeas call Alabama home. The state grows more hydrangeas in number and species than any other place in the world. Much of the credit for this botanical achievement goes to Eddie Aldridge, who dedicated his career to finding, cultivating, and spreading the beautiful and fragrant blooms to gardens everywhere. He discovered and patented the giant ball of flowers: the Snowflake Hydrangea. There is no better place to enjoy a late spring hydrangea tour than Eddie's personal garden, Aldridge Gardens, which he donated to the City of Hoover. The blooms display a wide spectrum of color and shape throughout the garden. Sculpture and other art graces nature's own palette. Events and classes enhance the experience of this free public garden.

530 Lorna Road, Hoover, 205-682-8019
www.aldridgegardens.com

BRAVE THE BEANSTALK
ATOP RED MOUNTAIN PARK

Red Mountain Park forms the western end of a future greenway stretching across Birmingham from end to end. This former mining site now reverberates not with blasting and hauling carts but with wind whispering in the trees and birds singing its praises. While there is plenty of nature to explore in its fifteen hundred acres, Red Mountain specializes in adventure. Scream down the zip line. Jump from one swinging platform to the next in the ropes course. Climb the Beanstalk tower. Bike along fifteen miles of trail. If the mountain trail appears daunting, take a Segway tour. Or relax with your four-footed friend at Remy's Dog Park. History also awaits at three historic iron ore mining sites at this free entry park.

2011 Frankfurt Drive, Birmingham, 205-202-6043
www.redmountainpark.org

THE PRESERVE
THE PEOPLE BUILT
AT RUFFNER MOUNTAIN

When the mines ceased, a coalition formed to save the mountain chaffed by mines and railroads, creating Ruffner Mountain Nature Preserve. While the scars and abandoned equipment rise above the forest floor, hardwoods and wildflowers effortlessly curl around the rust, bursting with their own pastels. A nature preserve, Ruffner restores habitat for all to enjoy the serenity and beauty of an Alabama woodland. A habitat garden showcases native plants and pollinators. Caves left by the mining efforts house hundreds of bats, making it a major hibernation site. A quarry reveals the ancient sea that once flowed through the limestone in its fossil record. Ruffner's 1,058 acres meander between Birmingham and Irondale, opening multiple entrances to trails for this free entry preserve.

1214 81st Street South, Birmingham, 205-833-8264
www.ruffnermountain.org

A BLOOMING GOOD TIME
AT THE BIRMINGHAM
BOTANICAL GARDENS

Walking the high path of the Wildflower Garden in early spring, you might think it snowed during the night; but no, the bloodroots are blooming! The scent of cherry blossoms fills the air in the renowned Japanese garden with an authentic tea house built by an honored master. Colors explode in the rhododendron garden. More than three thousand plant varieties flourish year-round in twenty-five garden collections. Always free, open 365 days from sunrise to sunset, the Birmingham Botanical Gardens serve as a perpetual oasis. Educational programs enhance the experience, with classes in native plants, herbs, flower arranging, pruning, gardening, and photography. Even the little ones can play with plants in a free, weekly Hikes for Tykes, available March through November. Check out the only public botanical library in the United States.

2612 Lane Park Road, Birmingham, 205-414-3950
www.bbgardens.org

A BOULDER WAY TO LIVE
AT MOSS ROCK PRESERVE

Rock climbers love the boulder field, and hikers love the forest and streams. As you enter Moss Rock Preserve, the large and varied boulders and outcroppings appeal to climbers of all skill levels. Many expert climbers cut their teeth on these ancient formations. For the casual hiker, the natural beauty engages the senses with waterfalls, wildlife, and the delicate scent of wildflowers in bloom. On a relatively short walk, you can pass through a hardwood forest, pine forest, open-brush habitat, and a wetland, all bursting with unique plants and wildlife. The shining star is a blazing star and a rare rayless goldenrod—a total of four rare species dwell on a type of sandstone glade found only in the northeast corridor of Alabama.

617 Preserve Parkway, Hoover
www.hooveral.org

Photo Credit:
Mark Peavy

MUSIC AND ENTERTAINMENT

HIGH CULTURE
DANCES, SINGS, AND PLAYS

Birmingham ranks as one of the few cities of its size to field high-quality symphony, ballet, and opera companies. The Alabama Symphony Orchestra pushes the boundaries with award-winning, artistically innovative, new American music. With fifty-four salaried musicians and an internationally acclaimed music director, the symphony performs 190 times per year. Occassionally, they play for performances of the Alabama Ballet, a nationally recognized company. The Alabama Ballet celebrates the holidays as one of only eight companies in the world permitted to perform Balanchine's Nutcracker®. Opera Birmingham annually fields a vocal competition where young national contenders launch careers. It recruits national talent to sing in performances and takes local vocal artists to the community in Opera Shots. If you hear opera in a bar, it's not the whiskey talking or singing—it's Opera Birmingham!

Alabama Symphony Orchestra
www.alabamasymphony.org/

Alabama Ballet
www.alabamaballet.org

Opera Birmingham
www.operabirmingham.org/

LOL IN REAL TIME
AT THE COMEDY CLUB

The great blizzard of 1993 might have been able to destroy the stage, but it could not stop the laughter. The Comedy Club StarDome survived and thrived and won the title of the number one comedy club in the country. From Positively Funny Improv to Open Mic Night, the StarDome features and nurtures local talent. National talent, from James Gregory to Colin Jost to NeNe Leakes and Henry Cho, regularly appear under the StarDome. At the new Star Bar, you can cozy up to your funny favorites as the entertainers join in the fun. There is hope for the humorously challenged. This family-owned club wants to tickle the Magic and offers classes to whip up your wit.

1818 Data Drive, Hoover, 205-444-0008
www.stardome.com

Photo Credit:
Mark Peavy

PRETEND YOU ARE
AT WORK FOR GUILT-FREE
ENTERTAINMENT AT WORKPLAY!

Original MTV DJ Alan Hunter came home to Birmingham with an idea: mixing work with play in a facility that provided creative space, a sound and video studio, a stage, and office space. WorkPlay's cabaret theater provides a three-hundred-seat venue for locally based national acts, such as Muscle Shoals Sound and the Blind Boys of Alabama; quirky acts, such as Kinky Friedman and the Texas Jewboys; and novel performers, such as Rockapella. Special series, like its songwriter series, keep audiences coming back to see what might be on the music menu. The setup allows for a comfortable seat at a table and a wide dance floor to keep moving. Check out its popular bar, and listen at the stage door to hear who might be playing.

500 23rd Street South, Birmingham, 205-380-4082
www.workplay.com

PERIODICALLY, YOU NEED A DRINK
AT THE COLLINS BAR

If you are a local, you can play the "Birmingham game" and try to recognize the names and places that replace chemical elements on the Periodic Table behind the bar. Some are obvious, such as the Cahaba River, while others are more obscure, for example, Merrilee, who formerly owned a renowned indie bar. If you flew in, you can enjoy the paper airplane décor. The art on the walls detail the steps for a perfect fold for these flying semi-wonders. As you contemplate the walls and ceiling, don't forget that the Collins Bar's true fame comes from its superb mixologists. The conversation starts with, "What do you like?" and the bartender takes it from there. With a backdrop of fine whiskeys, vodkas, Scotch, and bourbons, matched with fresh fruit purees, ginger beers, spices, and a bit of magic, the cocktails refresh and intoxicate the taste buds. Pair it with upscale comfort food.

2125 2nd Avenue North, Birmingham, 205-323-7995
www.thecollinsbar.com/

SATURN—
OUT OF THIS WORLD

He might be Brian Teasley or Birdstuff from Man or Astro Man? band fame, but he is definitely the founder of Saturn, an other-worldly music venue. Saturn, with a namesake rocket running through it, orbits outer space in the hip Avondale entertainment district. The space-themed club celebrates local jazz great Sun Ra, who claimed Saturn as a spiritual home, and the space race in Huntsville. The venue hosts experimental music, causes, trivia nights, and punk rock flea markets. Not all who come to play bring a guitar; you can pick your game from hundreds of selections, from Candy Land to vintage pinball and video games. The Satellite Bar provides two kinds of grains: beer and alcohol and the only all-you-can-eat cereal bar.

200 41st Street South, Birmingham, 205-703-9545
www.saturnbirmingham.com/

JUKE JOINT A JUMPIN'
AT GIP'S PLACE

It's one of the last, great juke joints. For more than sixty years, Henry "Gip" Gipson has hosted a party in his backyard every Saturday night, complete with rocking blues bands. Passing his ramshackle house, the end of the driveway transports you into a magical musical world. Christmas tree lights and tinsel illuminate the tin shack where the band plays. The soft glow grants mystical status even to the rusted-out lawn mower and dried-up paint cans. The smell of ribs and catfish infuse the grounds with irresistible scents of a Southern summer. The crowd settling in at old industrial spools and picnic tables ranges from the family emerging from the Mercedes, to the Harley-riders, to the neighbors. Imagine the best party you've ever gone to and you capture the feeling at Gip's.

3101 Avenue C, Bessemer, 205-919-8142

PARK YOURSELF IN THE GARAGE
FOR A GREAT TIME

In the early days of the automobile, chauffeurs sat by the phone in the garage awaiting a call from wealthy Highland Avenue families. In 1970, the neglected nooks designed for Model Ts were converted into stalls for small businesses, one of them a cafe. Soon, the cafe expanded, growing into one of the 10 Bars Worth Flying For in the world, according to *GQ*. An eclectic courtyard with scattered antiques,from pedestal sinks to sculpted cupids, the Garage Cafe sets the scene for great conversation, live music, and a cast of characters among the regulars (check out who is occupying the "asshole" seat at the bar). *Esquire* and other magazines have rated it as one of the best bars in America. The top time to stop in is when the wisteria vines bloom.

2304 10th Terrace South, Birmingham, 205-322-3220

BLAST OFF
IN THE ATOMIC LOUNGE

Feeling a little timid about meeting people at the bar? Express your inner feelings by ordering a chicken costume from the custom menu. Or, if confidence suits you better, order a Sex Panther drink and proudly slap on the temporary tattoo accompanying it. The Atomic Lounge indulges in Retro Futurism, a fondly remembered by-product of the space race. The 1960s have returned in full force with a fireplace reminiscent of *The Andy Griffith Show* and a living room set resembling *The Dick Van Dyke Show*. The turquoise sofa could make a match with Elvis' at Graceland. Set up like a midcentury modern home, this throwback bar returns to a comfort zone for boomers, where conversation flourished. Pick the room where you fit in. If you need more hominess, bring your old T-ball trophy and add it to the shelf.

2113 1st Avenue North, Birmingham, 205-983-7887
www.theatomiclounge.com

DRIVING YOU TO DRINK
IN OLD CAR HEAVEN

When men collect large items, such as, say, perhaps every Plymouth convertible car ever made, there comes a time when a home garage just isn't enough. The 46,000 square feet of Old Car Heaven beautifully displays the collection of Stewart Dudley's cars, with plenty of space left for dancing and socializing. The bar is open for happy hour Tuesday through Friday and grants you free rein to roam among the 111 rare cars. A popular rental space, check the event calendar for parties open to the public. If you fancy yourself as an old-car buff, you can make an appointment for a free tour of the 1920–1970 Chryslers, Dodges, and Plymouths, along with a 1915 Packard and a 1930s-era Brewster limousine. Every car stays in working order!

3501 1st Avenue. South, Birmingham, 205-326-8902
www.ochevents.com

STEEL AWAY
TO IRON CITY

A 1929 car dealership store shifted gears into one of Birmingham's most popular music venues. Iron City rocks with three concert stages, two bars, and a restaurant. The renovators kept the flavor of the light industrial site with metal accents, polished wood and stone, and earthbound colors. It books local, regional, and national bands for its 1,300 person (standing people) concert hall. On some nights, they show classic movies, such as sci-fi extravaganzas. For some events, for example when a comedian is booked, tables and chairs are set up for the performance. The secret to maximum comfort for many acts is to reserve a table in the mezzanine. The food and drinks equal the quality of the entertainment.

513 22nd Street South, Birmingham, 205-202-5483
www.ironcitybham.com

PARAMOUNT TO
A GOOD TIME

The Paramount is a throwback to when you played music in the garage, with a wall of car rims and vintage signs. If you were lucky, your garage housed a few games as well. A vintage mural gives a nod to the original Paramount, with people bustling beneath its sign. The Paramount arcade looks like a college bar from the 1970s, with classic pinball games, Ms. Pacman, and who could forget Donkey Kong? Don't be surprised to see families playing the games together in this family-friendly (until 9:00 p.m.) pub. Take some family photos in the old-fashioned photo booth. Children will happily eat the tasty burgers and hot dogs. The Alabama hummus, made from peanuts, tickles the taste buds as well.

200 20th Street North, Birmingham, 205-320-2824
www.paramountbirmingham.com

BREWS CRUISE,
IT'S PRETTY CRAFTY

When Avondale Brewing Company opened in an old brothel in a down-and-out neighborhood, it was soon brewing up success —for the 'hood, and for craft beer. Avondale was built on beer, but thrived on events, setting up outdoor music and food trucks. It is the home of the Wacky Tacky Light Tour every December, which more than 1,000 attend. They fired up a new entertainment district by drawing people in. They were soon followed by new craft makers: Cahaba Brewing Company, Trim Tab, Good People, and Ghost Train Brewing Company. These brewers launched Birmingham into the fastest-growing craft beer metro area in the United States. Over the mountain soon followed suit with Red Hills Brewing Company in Homewood. These five brewing companies offer bar service to taste their craft staples plus seasonal treats and flavor experiments. Each brewery presents its own beer, style, and personality.

Avondale Brewing Company
201 41st Street South, Birmingham, 205-777-5456
avondalebrewing.com

Cahaba Brewing Company
4500 5th Avenue South, Birmingham, 205-578-2616
www.cahababrewing.com

Trim Tab Brewing Company
2721 5th Avenue South, Birmingham, 205-703-0536
www.trimtabbrewing.com

Ghost Train Brewing Company
2616 3rd Avenue South, Birmingham, 205-201-5817
www.ghosttrainbrewing.com

Good People Brewing Company
114 14th Street South, Birmingham, 205-286-2337
www.goodpeoplebrewing.com

Red Hills Brewing Company
823 Central Avenue, Homewood, 205-582-2897
www.redhillsbrew.com

MOORISH FUN
AT THE ALABAMA THEATER

A Byzantine prince would feel quite at home in the Alabama
Theater, dubbed the Showplace of the South. Its Moorish
design exudes a magical charm necessary for a theater built as a
Paramount movie palace. It is a place where dreams dance across
the big screen and lovers kiss under exotic moons. Today, the big
screen reveals the true scope of such classics as *Gone with the
Wind* or *The Wizard of Oz*. Built for silent movies, the Mighty
Wurlitzer Organ rises from beneath the stage before every movie
for a sing-along with the audience. Ironically, the rare organ
saved the building as organ enthusiasts raised the preservation
funds. Concerts, operas, ballets, and other events fill the stage
for the 2,500 seats throughout the year.

817 Third Avenue North, Birmingham, 205-252-2262
www.alabamatheatre.com

TIP
The Alabama Theater should be seen in its original context—
as a movie hall. The Mighty Wurlitzer Organ was installed for silent
films. Check the website to view a real oldie for full effect.

A RETURN TO THE GOLDEN ERA
AT THE LYRIC THEATER

The Lyric once again rings with laughter and good times. The Marx Brothers, Mae West, Will Rogers, Sophie Tucker, and Milton Berle all walked the boards of the stage of this 1914 theater. Lovingly restored to the glory of its heyday, it shines as one of the few remaining examples of vaudeville theater—designed to bring the audience as close as possible to see and hear their favorite acts. Today, the Lyric stays booked up with bands, dancers, authors, comedians, and storytellers. The broad stage and intimate setting allow the performing arts to engage the audience. With the arching gold stage, the blue-and-gold box seats, and the mural above the stage, the sheer beauty of the Lyric sprinkles fairy dust on every performance.

1800 3rd Avenue North, Birmingham, 205-252-2262
www.lyricbham.com

KISS THE
MARBLE RING

Enter the TARDIS (the blue police phone booth from *Doctor Who*), dial the number, and be welcomed into the speakeasy world. Stuffed chairs and sofas in purple crushed velvet, a giant chandelier, and wallpaper that on closer examination reveals risqué figures, combine for 1920s glam. You are tempted to look around for Jay Gatsby. The first flapper, Alabama's Zelda Fitzgerald, inspired the room, the name, and the signature cocktails, each one highlighting her life. The obscure reference cursing someone to "die in the marble ring" is lost in Zelda's oft macabre expressions but suits the neo-Golden Age bar. The gem is hidden behind Hot Diggity Dogs, which you must walk through to get to the phone booth.

4028 5th Avenue South, Birmingham, 205-202-2252
www.themarblering.com

AT 2:00 A.M., WHERE DO YOU GO?
TO THE NICK!

Billed as "Birmingham's dirty little secret," this scruffy nightclub starts and ends late. It is the last to close: 4:00 a.m. on Thursday, 6:00 a.m. on the weekend. Known for the hottest music and coldest beer, the Nick has managed to stay hip for decades. On a given weekend, you may find a local favorite or a regional or national band screaming music past the pirate skull above the bar. They don't play favorites with genres. You could hear blues to bluegrass, rock to rockabilly, punk to pop, or hip-hop to rap. The music starts at 10:00 p.m. Even though the outside looks as if it is held up by old and new music posters, the Nick is here to stay.

2514 10th Avenue South, Birmingham, 205-252-3831
www.thenickrocks.com

REEL FUN
AT THE SIDEWALK FILM FEST

Film fans screen the newest documentaries, films, shorts, music, and animated films in some of the oldest venues. The Sidewalk Film Festival inhabits the historic theater district for six days in late August, showing a wide variety of films to a diverse audience. Both the Carver Theater and the Alabama were built with big screens for maximum viewing pleasure. Low-priced weekend passes urge attendees to take chances on challenging productions they might not otherwise see. The fresh, engaged audiences attract filmmakers from Alabama and beyond. Generally, the filmmakers attend the screening, giving commentary and answering audience questions. Running concurrently is SHOUT, the state's only film festival focusing on the lives, issues, and artists in the LGBTQ community.

www.sidewalkfest.com

HAVE A BLAST
AT SLOSS FEST

Ever seen a live iron pouring? A festival at a blast furnace museum can spark some surprises! The Sloss Metal Arts Program demonstrates the ironwork that made Birmingham. The Sloss Music & Arts Festival spans two days in July and squeezes in forty bands on four stages. Performers have included the Alabama Shakes, Widespread Panic, Death Cab for Cutie, St. Paul and the Broken Bones, and the Burning Peppermints. Billed as a lifestyle event, music ranks as only one of the arts presented here. Arts and crafts vary across genres for a diverse show of creativity. Iron isn't the only thing that will get poured. Try the custom cocktails, craft beers, and the great food to go with it.

20 32nd Street North, Birmingham, 205-254-2025
www.slossfest.com

GO COLONIAL
WITH NATIONAL SACRED HARP SINGING CONVENTION

Alabama is ground zero for Sacred Harp Singing. This three-hundred-plus-year-old choral tradition began in colonial America in singing schools teaching young people how to sight-read music. Sometimes called shape note singing, the hymnals use four distinct shapes of notes to indicate the sound. Uniquely democratic, the a cappella singing style places the singers in a hollow square with four vocal ranges facing each other, making an astonishing sound. Anyone can lead a song. The leader just enters the square, calls out a hymn number, and sings the first verse without words but using the fa-so-la sounds. The sacred harp refers to the voice—the one musical instrument everyone possesses. Anyone attending the singing is welcome to join the choir. People come from all over the world to hear old Alabama families sing the tradition carried on in small rural churches for generations.

www.fasola.org

SALUTE BIRMINGHAM
FOR STARTING VETERANS DAY
PARADES

At the end of World War II, a Birmingham veteran decided that Armistice Day, created to honor World War I soldiers, left out the newly returning soldiers, sailors, and airmen. Raymond Weeks gathered a delegation and created a proposal to present to President Dwight Eisenhower. He wanted to include all who have ever served in our military. In 1954, Eisenhower agreed and Veterans Day was born. Weeks led the first Veterans Day Parade in 1947 and every one thereafter until his death in 1985. The grand tradition continues with a new generation of men and women who walk the streets of Birmingham past cheering crowds in one of the largest veterans parades in the country.

www.nationalveteransday.org

GOING TO THE DOGS
ON DO DAH DAY

Has your dog ever expressed interest in wearing a pink tutu? Perhaps camo? Or maybe a Jedi knight costume? Do Dah Day truly goes to the dogs in this outrageous pet parade. Be sure to dress sharp—a doggie king and queen are crowned based on $1 votes. People decorate themselves, their cars/trucks, and pets. Floats roll and marching bands play in this canine mini-Mardi Gras. (No throws allowed; too many retrievers!) During the day, the historic Highland parks are filled with bands, food wagons, and people and pets grooving to the sounds. It's all in good fun for this annual fund-raiser for local animal shelters. Look for the annual event around the third week in May.

www.dodahday.org

MAGIC CITY ART CONNECTION
BRIDGING PEOPLE TO ART

For three days every April, art takes over. Linn Park, in the heart of downtown, transforms into a multifaceted art show. Magic City Art Connection is Birmingham's largest festival, with two hundred artists exploding with creativity and thousands who come to appreciate their work. The competition is juried, attracting major artists. The great majority are visual artists, but the other arts appear in dances and musical performances. The sensual experience is completed with alluring aromas of special tastings. Food vendors bring their favorites and their most innovative fare. Complete the sensory experience by touching the sculpture installations. This festival propelled Birmingham into Top Ten Best Downtowns in 2014 by Livability.com. Stroll through the park engaging fully in art.

Linn Park, 710 20th Street North, Birmingham
www.magiccityart.com

SAVING THE PLANET WHILE MAKING ART
AT THE MOSS ROCK FESTIVAL

Self-named an eco-creative festival, the Moss Rock Festival tours you through artists booths and also through the Preserve. Moss Rock, home to rare and endangered species, borders the community and the park where the festival is held. While very few festivals take you away from vendors, this festival wants to save the earth and make it more beautiful. Guided hikes and yoga trekking are scheduled throughout the day with community naturalists. Environmental groups man booths alongside those of the artists. On Artists Row, a hundred artists display artwork primarily inspired by nature. Through the cross section of mediums, many of them will use natural or repurposed materials. Music and children's activities throughout the November weekend appeal to a diverse range of ages and families.

617 Preserve Parkway, Hoover
www.mossrockfestival.com

SHHHH...
SECRET STAGES

More than sixty bands will grace the stages, making Secret Stages not so secret. Secret Stages took up the banner of indie music and up-and-coming new artists who are seeking an audience. Fans pour into town to hear new tunes, making Birmingham a well-rounded music destination. Local band St. Paul and the Broken Bones launched here and credits the spotlight of Secret Stages for it propulsion onto the national scene. Secret Stages often discovers new talent on the verge of acclaim. The bands play in a two-block radius of downtown Birmngham, making it easy to stage hop. The two-day festival takes over the Loft District the first weekend in August.

www.secretstages.net

PARTY WITH GUSTO
AT THE GREEK FESTIVAL

During the rush to build the Magic City, Greek immigrants poured into the new city. Many of them opened restaurants, many still owned by their descendants. Every September the food and music draw thousands to the Holy Cross–Holy Trinity Greek Orthodox Cathedral Greek Festival. It's a thoroughly Greek party in mid-September, with all the exuberance brought from the old country in full force on the parking lot stage. Church members dance, play music, and sing in the Greek tradition, with children's performances especially charming. Meanwhile, long lines of people queue up for tasty meals. With so many restaurateurs, the church serves an astounding array of traditional dishes and even mans a drive-through window. In the makeshift shop area, authentic Greek and Mediterranean gifts and Christian souvenirs are available for purchase.

307 19th Street South, Birmingham, 205-716-3088
www.birminghamgreekfestival.net

EMBRACE YOUR INNER TACKY
AT THE WACKY TACKY CHRISTMAS LIGHT TOURS

Come dressed as Cousin Eddie. Or Mrs. Claus. Wear your tackiest Christmas sweater. Hop on the bus to see the best of the worst and the wackiest Christmas light displays! Join Fresh Air Family for this anti–Norman Rockwell Christmas tradition— the Wacky Tacky Christmas Light Tour. More than a thousand people annually load up on buses for a guided tour of over-the-top Christmas displays. And other holidays—see the Hanukkah House, where they took a Joy to the World and wacked off the "J." Or Santa's Trailer Park, where giant mooning Santas greet you on the walking path. It is a tactacular event that raises scholarship money for children and youth to go to Gross Out Camp, an award-winning science camp.

www.wackytacky.org

Photo Credit:
Mark Peavy Photography

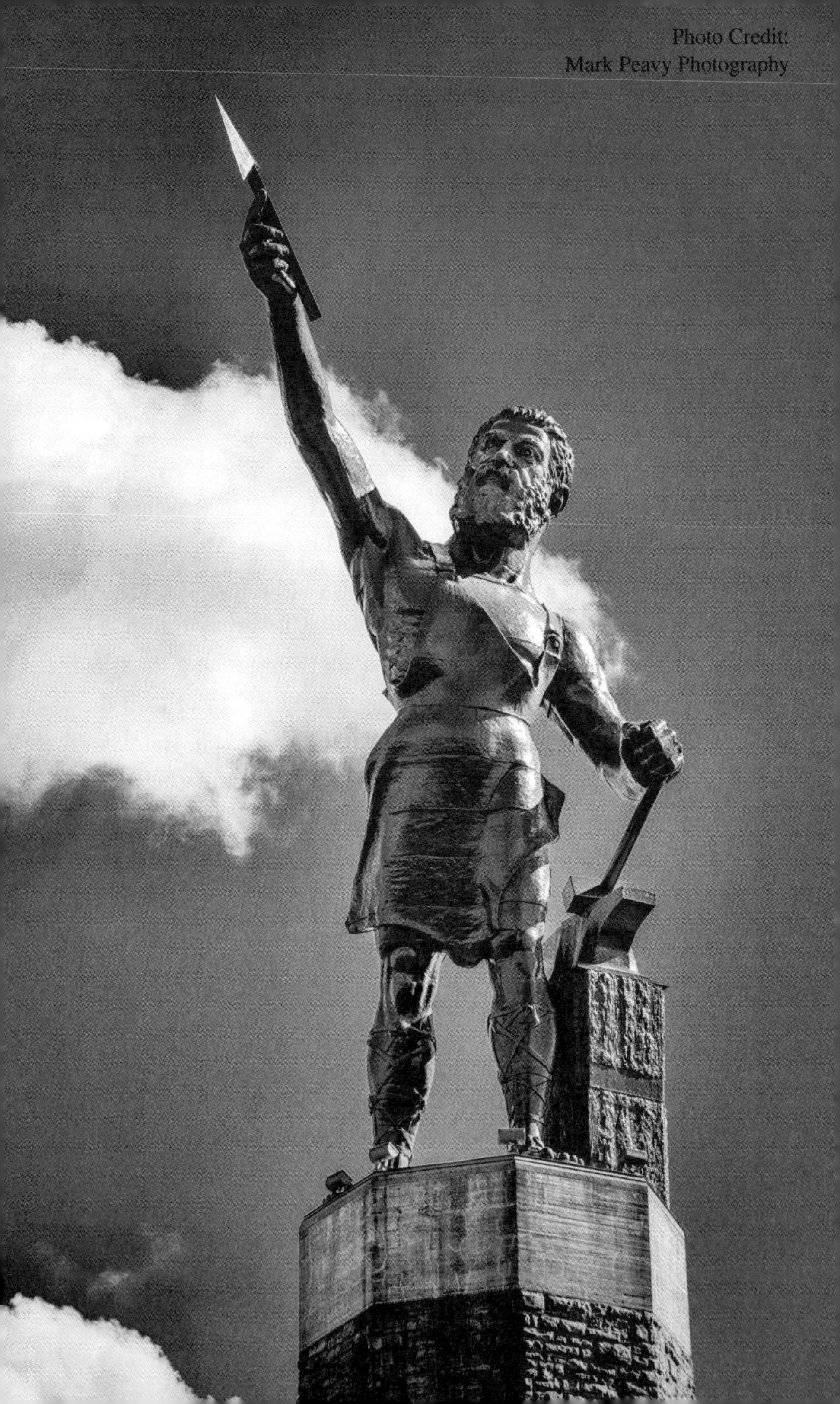

CULTURE AND HISTORY

BIRMINGHAM'S ANTEBELLUM PAST
AT ARLINGTON

A sword hangs in a case, a testimony to love. The Civil War soldier dug his sword into a tree, declaring his undying love to his weeping betrothed, as long as the sword remained. He never returned. The red iron ore throughout Birmingham colors the soil, creating poor farm land so few plantations existed in the area. Arlington Antebellum Home & Gardens stands as the last reminder of the Old South. The Greek Revival home showcases nineteenth century decorative arts with furniture, textiles, silver, and paintings. The garden is planted with heirloom plants. An early owner, William S. Mudd, may be related to the notorious Dr. Mudd who reset the leg of John Wilkes Booth. The house was occupied by Union Major General James H. Wilson, who spared it from the soldier's torch, because Mudd was a fellow Mason.

331 Cotton Avenue, Southwest, Birmingham, 205-780-5656
www.arlingtonantebellumhomeandgardens.com

STORIES COME ALIVE
AT OAK HILL CEMETERY

Meet Louise Wooster, the colorful madam who saved the young city of Birmingham during a cholera epidemic. Or greet Charles Linn, a city pioneer, who wanted to wake up on judgment day looking out over the greatest industrial city in the South. Perhaps famous murder victims Emma, May, and Irene Hawes haunt the cemetery, looking for the husband/father who committed a sensational crime in 1888. Oak Hill Cemetery frequently offers guided tours on Saturdays to introduce visitors to Birmingham's buried history. In the fall, around Halloween, the dead come to life with local actors embodying the most fascinating residents of the city's first cemetery. In June, it hosts a film festival featuring historic reels and independent movies.

120 19th Street North, Birmingham, 205-251-6532
www.oakhillbiringham.com

TRACE THE ROAD TO FREEDOM
ON THE CIVIL RIGHTS TRAIL

It began at Bethel, which starts the story of the Birmingham Civil Rights Movement, a historic struggle fought in the streets, parks, and churches. Reverend Fred Shuttlesworth championed rights from the pulpit of Bethel and sought help from Dr. Martin Luther King, Jr., a fellow pastor from Montgomery. Their leadership clashed with Jim Crow advocates to dramatic effect, bringing about an end to segregation laws. Reminders of the struggle can be seen in Kelly Ingram Park, where statues capture the fire hoses, dog attacks, jailed children, praying pastors, and Dr. King. Across the street, the Birmingham Civil Rights Institute (BCRI) leads you from displays of a segregated world to today's struggle for human rights. Across from the BCRI stands the 16th Street Baptist Church, where protest songs pierced the air, speeches inspired marchers, and the Children's March poured out of the sanctuary. In a final act of depravity, a bomb ended the lives of four little girls, sparking the passage of the Civil Rights Act. The area was designated a national monument by President Barack Obama in 2017.

www.heritagetrail.birminghamal.gov

Birmingham Civil Rights Institute
520 16th Street North, Birmingham,
205-328-9696
www.bcri.org

Bethel Baptist Church
3200 28th Avenue North, Birmingham,
205-322-5360
www.bethelcollegeville.org

16th Street Baptist Church
1530 6th Avenue North, Birmingham,
205-251-9402
www.16thstreetbaptist.org

TIP
Start your exploration of the Civil Rights Trail at Bethel Baptist Church.
Call ahead to book their historian for a tour. She lived through the
struggle and shares her personal experience to help you understand the
climate that birthed the Civil Rights Movement.

A GIFT FOR YOUR EYES
AT THE BIRMINGHAM MUSEUM OF ART

The ever-inspiring Renaissance launched a new art museum when twenty-nine Italian paintings from the Samuel H. Kress Foundation were first exhibited here in 1952. The Birmingham Museum of Art has since grown to house more than twenty-six thousand art objects, making it one of the finest regional museums in the country. Its holdings span from ancient to modern works, with a broad cultural diversity from Asia, Europe, Africa, and the Americas. Decorative arts embellish its collection with what is considered the nation's finest collection of Vietnamese ceramics, plus superior collections of English ceramics and French furniture. A local couple provided the perfect addition: the largest collection of Wedgwood outside of England, beautifully interpreted in its displays. The museum is owned by the City of Birmingham, allowing free entry for all who want to experience it. Education programs offer lectures, music, classes, special events, and artist presentations.

2000 Rev. Abraham Woods, Jr. Boulevard, Birmingham, 205-254-2565
www.artsbma.org

PREPARE FOR A SENSORY OVERLOAD
AT JOE MINTER'S YARD

Protest signs and Jesus mix comfortably in the African Village created by artist Joe Minter. Sculptures, shrines, wooden plaques, and baby dolls in his urban yard tell the story of his people, from the arrival on slave ships to modern-day police abuse. The stories emerge with the help of work gloves, car parts, bicycle chains, metal frames, wood, and Christmas decorations. The famed folk artist crafts moving testimonies to the struggle for equality and the importance of his Christian faith. A stroll through the maze of yard art combines a sensory experience of beauty and thought. Even the art cannot compare with meeting the artist himself, a fascinating free spirit and creative mind working on "orders from God."

931 Nassau Avenue Southwest, Birmingham, 205-322-7370
www.facebook.com/joeminterafricanvillage

VULCAN,
THE GOD OF THE FORGE
WATCHES OVER US

Towering above the city, Vulcan perpetually examines the spear he just pulled from the forge. As the world's largest cast-iron statue, Vulcan emerged from the forge himself in 1904. He was created by city leaders for the 1904 World's Fair in St. Louis, crafted to represent the young steel town. He captured the Grand Prize in the Palace of Mines and Metallurgy. He returned to the city of his birth in pieces. Due to his bare backside, the ladies of Birmingham rebuffed attempts to erect him in a downtown park. He spent several years at the Alabama State Fairgrounds before a Works Progress Administration project built his sandstone pedestal atop Red Mountain. Today, visitors can ride to the top of his base for a panoramic view of the area. A museum tracks the history of Vulcan and the city that created him.

1701 Valley View Drive, Birmingham, 205-933-1409
www.visitvulcan.com

EXPERIMENT
AT THE MCWANE SCIENCE CENTER

An old, shuttered department store reemerged as the McWane Science Center in downtown Birmingham. Since opening in 1998, millions of people have visited the center, stretching out on a bed of nails, touching live sting rays, and staring into the gaping mouth of an Alabama Mosasaur, the most feared prehistoric sea monster. As the site of an ancient ocean and swamps teaming with life, Alabama hides more dinosaur bones beneath its surface than any other state east of the Mississippi. At McWane, you can see dinosaur bones and fossils found nearby. The Itty Bitty Magic City spurs creative learning in preschool children. Along the way, children can explore space, bubbles, the science of the whish of a basketball, and antigravity. Education programs engage guests with experiments and demonstrations. The IMAX Dome Theater plays documentaries using technology that brings the audience into the action.

200 19th Street North, Birmingham, 205-714-8300
www.mcwane.org

HAVE A BLAST
AT SLOSS FURNACES

In the hills surrounding Birmingham, the fires from Sloss Furnaces would light up the night sky. From 1882 to 1971, Sloss Furnaces produced pig iron, so-called because of the shallow connectors between the molds, giving it the appearance of a pig's tail. These furnaces produced twenty-four thousand tons of high-quality iron the first year. Birmingham is one of the only places in the world where everything you need to make steel is found within thirty miles. Colonel James Sloss helped found the Magic City with his railroad connections and new blast furnaces. When the operation shut down, the city moved to develop the site into the only preserved blast furnace in the United States. Now a National Historic Landmark, you can explore Sloss with self-guided tours. Watch out for ghosts! Sloss often hosts concerts, cookoffs, and paranormal events from ghost stories to ghostbusting investigations.

20 32nd Street North, Birmingham, 205-254-2025
www.slossfurnaces.com

TAKE OFF
AT THE SOUTHERN MUSEUM OF FLIGHT

No one believed African-American men could fly airplanes during World War II until the Tuskegee Airmen proved them wrong. See the story of these brave and pioneering pilots in an exhibition at the Southern Museum of Flight. The disastrous Bay of Pigs invasion in 1961 took the lives of four men from the Alabama Air National Guard. Sixty men from Alabama trained Cuban exiles for an invasion of Cuba. These men are honored in the Aviation Hall of Fame in the Southern Museum of Flight. Other exhibits include Vietnam-era helicopters, Korean War jets, and crop dusters. Throughout the museum, you can see memorabilia from military, civilian, and experimental aircraft from the earliest days of powered flight to modern times.

4343 73rd Street North, Birmingham, 205-833-8226
www.southernmuseumofflight.org

FEEL YOUNG AGAIN
AT SAMUEL ULLMAN MUSEUM

A former Confederate soldier, Samuel Ullman fought for the rights of African-American children to receive the same education as whites. Serving on Birmingham's first school board, he also argued for equal pay for black teachers. The German-born Jew served as a lay rabbi for Temple Emanu-El, a reform congregation, but he is most famous for his retirement occupation as a poet. In 1918, at the age of seventy-eight, he penned the poem "Youth," a testament to optimism and youthful outlook. A framed copy of the poem hung in the office of one of Ullman's biggest fans, General Douglas MacArthur, when he was stationed in Japan. The war-weary Japanese embraced the poem as they began to rebuild their country. The former Ullman residence was opened in 1994 by the Japan-America Society of Alabama and the University of Alabama at Birmingham.

2150 15th Avenue, South, Birmingham, 205-910-3876
www.uab.edu/ullmanmuseum

NO TUXEDO REQUIRED
AT THE ALABAMA JAZZ HALL OF FAME

In Birmingham, Tuxedo Junction was a place immortalized forever by a song cowritten by Alabama Jazz Hall of Fame honoree Erskine Hawkins. His legendary Parker High School teacher John T. "Fess" Whatley provided a feeder school for bands such as Duke Ellington and Count Basie. More than a dozen famed jazz musicians, graduated from his program. One of his students, the eccentric Herman "Sun Ra" Blount, formed his Intergalactic Space Arkestra. Jazz greats with ties to Alabama include Montgomery's Nat King Cole, Florence's W.C. Handy, Troy's Clarence "Pinetop" Smith, and Birmingham's Lionel Hampton. The Art Deco Carver Theater in the Civil Rights District houses the collection of artifacts. A living museum, music often rings through the Carver by way of jazz jam sessions, concerts, classes, and dances.

1631 4th Avenue North, Birmingham, 205-327-9424
www.jazzhall.com

PERFECTION MADE PERFECT
AT VIRGINIA SAMFORD THEATRE

The opening curtain rose in 1927 for what is now known as the Virginia Samford Theatre in Caldwell Park. After too many of its actors departed for World War II it closed, reopening in 1950 as Town and Gown, led by the legendary James Hatcher. He demanded that every hand hit the same level and every knee bend at the same angle. This larger-than-life character developed local talent into Broadway and film careers, most notably actress and author Fannie Flagg. Today, the historic theater continues to offer a broad range of dance, music, and theater performances. In keeping with the Hatcher philosophy, the theater educates young people in the art and discipline of the stage. From classics to new works, the theater both challenges and entertains through art.

1116 26th Street. South, Birmingham, 205-251-1206
www.virginiasamfordtheatre.org

THE EDGE OF YOUR SEAT
AT BIRMINGHAM FESTIVAL THEATRE

Three young thespians rebelled against the traditional Hatcher theater in 1972, seeking greater creative freedom. One of them was Carl Stewart, who recently retired from Terrific New Theater. In their first season, they burst onto the scene with productions challenging the status quo, from race, gender, and sexuality to the myths of the nuclear family. The intimate theater, carved out of a loading dock, has since staged more than 250 productions seen by more than one hundred thousand people. Birmingham's longest continuously operating community theater, Birmingham Festival Theatre spans from new wave to classics in its repertoire, with the city's finest talent. The productions continue to inspire with edgy new or rarely performed productions, along with original debuts from local writers. This historic theater, keeps the laughter and the tears rolling in this quaint setting.

1901½ 11th Avenue South, Birmingham, 205-933-2383
www.bftonline.org

EXPLOSIVE HUMOR AND PATHOS
AT TNT—TERRIFIC NEW THEATRE

Theatre patrons in need of a good laugh have depended on the creative players at Terrific New Theatre since 1986. Buried in each chuckle are thought-provoking concepts that entertain through gender-bending roles, absurdity, and/or those familiar Southern family landscapes. Modern Southern playwrights have found a home for innovative works at TNT, founded by Carl Stewart, who also founded Birmingham Festival Theatre. Thursday nights, with the exception of opening night, offer plays for new audiences with its "pay what you can afford" policy. If you show up for a show without a ticket, a "walk-in" horn announces your spontaneity. Stewart retired in 2016, and artistic director Tam DeBolt, plans to continue the serious side of often laugh-out-loud contemporary theater located in the heart of Pepper Place.

2821 2nd Avenue South, Suite A, Birmingham, 205-328-0868
www.terrificnewtheatre.com

PUT A SONG IN YOUR HEART
AT RED MOUNTAIN THEATRE

Patsy Cline, the Lennon Sisters, and Tevye from *Fiddler on the Roof* have all been given voice at Red Mountain Theatre Company. This venue recruits Tony winners to perform alongside local talent and acting students, merging them into thrilling performances. Here, local writers debut new works and up-and-coming directors hone their craft. A season could include everything from an old favorite to a challenging new work. One of the goals of the theater is to engage the community with both thought-provoking art and also a place to escape the problems of life with a song, a dance, and a laugh or two. With an active education program, Red Mountain Theatre pulls from an impressive talent pool of its own making.

2900 1st Avenue South, Birmingham, 205-324-2424
www.redmountaintheatre.org

SHOPPING AND FASHION

FOR BIRMINGHAM'S HIPPEST HIPSTERS
AT OPEN SHOP

Look for the fake book backs in the window to find this hidden jewel in Woodlawn. Open Shop, a music and clothing store, started with a unisex fashion focus and soon broke out into clothing for one and all. From the latest in high-top tennis shoes to workman jackets, this shop serves your hipster needs. One rack offers shirts and jackets made from vintage recycled material. Don't be surprised if you see a lapel at the bottom or a pocket on the shoulder. They feature a small selection of novel fashions, such as 1.61, whose cofounder is Alabama native Kimberley Wesson. Wesson, a University of Alabama at Birmingham grad, designs a pant-based, uniform, unisex look geared to inspiring self-confidence in the wearer. Libertine's line of deconstructed and recycled materials fill the side rack.

5529 1st Avenue South, Birmingham

EVERY ITEM TELS A STORY
AT CLUB DUQUETTE

Musicians, artists, and designers, Duquette and Morgan Johnston perform at every level and have now brought their eclectic interests to a brick-and-mortar shop in Woodlawn. Each item in Club Duquette comes with a story: a fifteen-year-old from Rainbow City who started his own leather crafting company; a woman returning to her family factory roots by making Alabama socks; a perfume company out of California using only wildcrafted ingredients; and a French knife company still using two-hundred-year-old manufacturing techniques. Great Bear Beard Wax Co. tips its head to hipster facial fancies. The heart of the store springs from the creative minds of the owners, who also run Rugged & Fancy designs. Duquette designs T-shirts, and Morgan designs jewelry and custom clothes, such as vintage military-style jackets.

17 55th Place South, Birmingham

THEADORA,
A TALE OF TWO SISTERS

Two sisters set out to bring new and little-known designers to the local fashion scene in 1994. Today, Theadora stands for cool, casual clothes brought to Birmingham from around the globe. While they stick with some traditional standbys, the mix brings in cult labels and indie outsiders. Lines such as Alice & Trixie (named for an old Jackie Gleason skit) focuses on bohemian glam style culled from vintage style. RU eschews romance for the strong woman and views the body as an architectural challenge. Theadora's owners see both women, and all in between, with an eye for everyone's unique beauty. With a line of accessories and shoes, Theadora can design a total look to suit your figure and flair, and ship it to your door.

2821 18th Street South, Homewood, 205-879-0335
www.theadora.com

SHAIA'S OF HOMEWOOD,
OLD-WORLD SHOPPING
ELEGANCE FOR MEN

With an old-world leather sofa and chairs surrounded by sharp suits and shoes, you get the feeling you might have stepped into Jay Gatsby's dressing room. The warm atmosphere sets a tone more akin to a men's club than a retail shop. Indeed, men bring their sons here to teach them proper dress. Founded in 1922, a fourth generation of Shaia's recently added a concept shop devoted to fashion geared for a younger crowd. Armani and all the classics can be found along with a few upstarts. Esquire routinely names it in the Best of Class list. The upscale shop can design and create everything from a custom-fit suit to a travel wardrobe to a new home closet to accommodate your threads of investment. Jay Gatsby, indeed.

818 18th Street South, Homewood, 205-871-1312
www.shaias.com

SPRINKLED WITH FAIRY DUST
AND WHITE FLOWERS

Owners Eric and Diana Hanson fell in love with a magic garden created by artists who first lived in their home. More than just flowers bloomed for this artist and photographer; they began designing custom T-shirts that flourished in the rich soil of showrooms. Soon, they opened their own shop, White Flowers, to showcase their own designs, from baby clothes to tea towels. Entering White Flowers evokes every girl's fantasy of a fairy cottage. Sculptures, drawings, dried flowers, gauzy towers—all in white—tempt you to listen for the galloping of Prince Charming's steed. Clever sayings dot the T-shirts and towels with wisdoms such as "Wildflowers grow where they will and come back year after year, like a forever friend."

2800 18th Street South, Homewood, 205-871-4640
www.whiteflowers.com

SOUTHERN-STYLE GLAM
AT GUS MAYER

If you are going to a Southern bridal tea, shop at Gus Mayer's for the perfect summer party dress. It will be simple, exquisite, and well-fitted. Helpful clerks will dash about to find alluring accessories. The upscale store opened in 1900 and remains a family-owned business. Gus Mayer isn't just for special occasions. A contemporary collection takes you to the picnic or the ball field to watch Little League. The store presents a study of Birmingham itself, the dichotomy of a Chanel suit with matching hat and a shaggy vest for date night. In between, jewelry, shoes, and cosmetics complete the fashion picture. And you can pick up a perfectly appropriate wedding gift to take to the tea.

225 Summit Boulevard, Suite 700, Birmingham, 205-870-3300
www.gusmayer.com

FLASH FASHION FORWARD
AT ETC...

This fashion-forward shop brings in clothing from top designers around the world—and from next door. Birmingham's Liz Legg might mix a mammoth bone or a less-ancient Roman coin with raw geodes. Or find vintage Hermes or Rolex. Cathy Waterman, Armenta, Moritz Glik, Monique Pean, Spinelli Kilcollin, and Hoorsenbuhs bring everything from diamonds to bangles. In clothing, a feminine and flirty Rodarte can be polished off with a Golden Goose silver sneaker or a colorful midtop sporting a purple star. Knit wear, ever ready to go on an island retreat or a stop at the carpool line, comes in unique pieces from Raquel Allegra, Inhabit, Proenza Schouler, and the Great. Fashion at Etc... re-creates itself daily.

2726 Cahaba Road, Mountain Brook, 205-871-6747
www.shopetcjewelry.com

EVERY BOOK IS SIGNED
AT THE ALABAMA BOOKSMITH

Only one bookstore in our known literary universe offers only books signed by the author, Alabama Booksmith. A veteran bookseller from generations of booksellers, owner Jake Reiss transformed a normal bookshop with stuffed racks of books into a collector's dream. Armed with the knowledge that the true book collector focuses on first editions and signed copies, Jake grants the desires of his bookworm patrons. The unique model emphasizing the personal touch shows every book's face—no spine shopping here! While people from all fifty states and all over the world order the signed copies, locals can take their books right from the hand of the author. More than a thousand authors have made the pilgrimage to Alabama Booksmith for the packed signing events.

2626 19th Place South, Homewood 205-870-4242
www.alabamabooksmith.com

VINYL NEVER WENT OUT OF STYLE
AT CHARLEMAGNE RECORD EXCHANGE

Go in well armed if you plan to stump Jimmy Griffin on recorded music. Customers don't bother googling music they might just vaguely remember since it is faster to ask Jimmy—and he can even tell you if somebody else made a better recording of it. A walking encyclopedia of vinyl and beyond, Jimmy can pluck the most obscure artist out of a packed record stack. When you climb the stairs to the Five Points store, you enter a shaggy version of the 1970s. The only thing missing is eight-track tapes. The store is small on space but high on volume and higher on service. You can find everything from Ravi Shankar to Beyoncé to vintage Andy Griffith comedy albums, with Jimmy as your laser pointer.

1924½ 11th Avenue South, Birmingham, 205-322-5349

PUT SOME CLOTHES
ON NAKED ART

Naked Art refers to the "naked eye," not the look of shock. All seventy artists sharing space are considered "not yet famous," although a few have gained significant fame for their creations, such as John Lytle Wilson. The time to go is on a monthly third Friday, when the shops in the Forest Park neighborhood open their doors in the evening and welcome you with libations and snacks. In the colorful gallery, artists mingle their works so that paintings hang over clothing and hats tower over jewelry. The selection crosses every genre, from fine art to found objects, from fabrics to metal works, from jewelry to pottery. The items tend to be smaller, with a goal of making functional art accessible for every budget.

3831 Clairmont Avenue, Birmingham, 205-595-3553
www.nakedartusa.com

FROM BUTTER TO LEATHER
AT PEPPER PLACE

If you know which space to visit, you can enter the vault where the top-secret Dr. Pepper recipe was secured. This former industrial site has morphed into decorator shopping, restaurants, a theater, and a weekend market. While you enjoy the live music and munch on fresh-baked muffins, stroll through makers booths displaying leather, beadwork, tie-dye, batik, art, pottery, and clothes. You can purchase everything from a watermelon to a bar of soap to a dining room table to a painting. The Saturday-only Pepper Place Market launched as a place to find quality produce and evolved into a weekend staple for entertainment, shopping, and visiting with neighbors. Be sure to bring Fido. Fetch provides an ice cream truck for dogs. During the week, Pepper Place merchants sell designer furnishings, plants and garden tools and offer grooming services.

2829 2nd Avenue South, Birmingham
www.pepperplacemarket.com
www.pepperplace.com

REED BOOKS
AND MUSEUM
OF FOND MEMORIES

When Jim Reed's wife decided that the living room should be a place where people could actually sit, she banished her husband's book obsession into what is now Reed's Books and Museum of Fond Memories. A confessed hoarder, Jim divides people into keepers and tossers, landing solidly in the keeper lane. His quirky collection resembles a combination of yard sale and an old bachelor who was never really housebroken. Spending an hour or two with Jim floods the senses with memories and chuckles and the sense that his shop holds a significant percentage of the world's knowledge. Books range from new to five hundred years old. Things range from a giant Porky Pig to vintage lava lamps. If you seek a book, no matter how obscure, Jim can root it out for you.

2021 3rd Avenue North, Birmingham, 205-326-4460
www.jimreedbooks.com

PURCHASE THE PAST
ON THE ALABAMA ANTIQUE TRAIL

Follow the Alabama Antique Trail with stores for every taste and style. Birmingham is studded with antique stores to fill historic homes and new construction popping up around the city. Some focus on midcentury (Avondale Antiques), while others focus on repurposing in unique ways (Junky to Funky). Some are a collection of sellers, each with a personality all its own (Urban Suburban). Others create shabby chic by transforming the humble into the spectacular (Oak Mountain Emporium). Collectibles rule in shops such as What's on 2nd. The grande dame of antique shops is Hannah's Antique Mall, with thirty-five massive cases of jewelry, silver, and collectibles, plus twenty-seven thousand square feet of European and American antiques. The Alabama Antique Trail compiled a list to make it easy to buy memories. Pick up a Trail brochure at any of the shops.

www.alabamaantiquetrail.com

A CITY STORE OLDER
THAN THE CITY—BROMBERG'S

The Bromberg family opened their first store before Birmingham was incorporated as a city, making it older than the place it calls home. It is one of the oldest family businesses in America. Opening in 1836, Bromberg's third generation brought the finer things of life to a sleepy town bursting into the Magic City. Bromberg's primarily deals in diamonds and fine jewelry, putting rings on the fingers of thousands of hopeful brides and happy wives. Don't see what you like? The master jeweler can design your dream ring. Once the wedding is set, the gift section helps those who are invited to the happy occasion. Watches, rings, earrings, necklaces, and trained staff make happy occasion or "I'm sorry" shopping easy.

Downtown, The Summit, Mountain Brook Village
www.brombergs.com

GET YOUR PEANUTS
AT THE PEANUT DEPOT

The rich scent of fresh roasted peanuts permeates the air even before you enter the building. The Peanut Depot cranks up its antique roasting machines and transforms the average peanut into a delicacy. Just seeing the old machines at work is worth the visit. For more than a hundred years, this company has been honoring the tradition of preparing peanuts without oils or preservatives, making them a healthy, flavorful snack. Three flavors emerge from the fire: fresh roasted, salted, and Cajun. Depending on your peanut addiction, you can buy a bag of peanuts for yourself, your family, or your stadium. Choose your bag: plastic, burlap, or gift-wrapped for a friend.

3009 Messer Airport Highway, Birmingham, 205-251-3314
www.peanutdepot.com

THIS DANDE'
LION PURRS

It's a tale of Joan, Joann, and Joanne—each representing a new generation of Dande' Lion ladies. Opened in 1969 by the first Joan, the shop focused on timeless styles that still keep the shop in vogue. Like her great-aunt Joan, Joanne sees her friends coming in for wedding and special occasion gifts. In Birmingham, it is a right of passage to list your china preferences at the Dande' Lion prior to other vows. Whether you are looking for an avocado plate or an egg coddler, nothing is too specialized in the way of interiors. Antiques, furniture, lamps, vases, and linens mix comfortably with Roll Tide and War Eagle items. The three ladies follow the mantra: buy what you like and your customers will like it, too.

2701 Culver Road, Mountain Brook, 205-879-0691

SUGGESTED
ITINERARIES

THE GREAT OUTDOORS

Canoe the Cahaba, 48

Hiking at Ruffner Mountain, 57

Climb the Beanstalk at Red Mountain, 55

Orienteering at Oak Mountain, 50

Mountain biking at Oak Mountain, 50

Bouldering at Moss Rock Preserve, 59

Stroll through the Birmingham Botanical Gardens, 58

Walk around Aldridge Gardens, 53

Play Frisbee at Railroad Park, 51

Play a game at Avondale Park, 52

FOR THE GULF SEAFOOD LOVER

The crab cakes at Highland's Bar & Grill, 3

Pan-seared scallops at Hot and Hot Fish Club, 4

Everything at the Fish Market, 14

Seafood gumbo at the Bright Star, 19

Seafood platter at Niki's West, 13

Fried oysters at Café Dupont, 6

Pan-roasted Gulf black grouper at Satterfield's, 18

FOR THE VEGETARIAN

Veggie bowl at Feast and Forest, 8

Meat-free cooked vegetables on Niki's steam table, 13

Mushroom burger at Woodlawn Cycle Café, 7

Spanakopita and falafels at Nabeel's, 22

Fried green tomatoes at Irondale Café, 15

Ethiopian at Pizitz Food Hall, 9

Goat in the orchard at Chez Lulu, 10

Tofu dog or vegan chili at Hot Diggity Dog, 24

Veggies at Lloyd's, 16

Red beans and rice at Johnny's, 21

Blackeye peas with okra at Eagle's (note: their spelling for peas), 17

Famed tomato salad at Hot and Hot, 4

Baked grits Highland's, 3

FOR COCKTAILS

Collins Bar, 66

Paramount, 73

Atomic Lounge, 70

Old Car Heaven, 71

The Marble Ring, 79

WorkPlay!, 65

Saturn, 67

Iron City, 72

Highlands Bar, 3

MUSEUM LOVER

Birmingham Museum of Art, 98

Negro Southern Leagues Museum, 46

Birmingham Civil Rights Museum, 96

Ullman Museum, dedicated to a Jewish Civic leader and poet, 104

Barber Motorsports Museum, 41

International Motorsports Hall of Fame, 38

Sloss Furnances, 102

Arlington House, 94

Southern Museum of Flight, 103

Vulcan Museum, 100

Jazz Hall of Fame, 105

DOWNTOWN

Reed Books, 123

Pizitz Food Hall, 9

Collins Bar, 66

Paramount, 73

Railroad Park, 51

Regions Field, 45

Birmingham Museum of Art, 98

McWane Center, 101

Café Dupont, 6

Alabama Theater, 77

Lyric Theater, 78

Feast and Forest, 8

ONLY IN BIRMINGHAM

FAMILY FUN

DATE NIGHT

Birmingham Festival Theatre, 107

Red Mountain Theatre, 109

The biggest movie night ever at the Alabama Theater's big screen, 77

9 pm ride up the elevator for a city from atop Vulcan, 100

Late night? The Nick, 80

FREE ENTERTAINMENT

Birmingham Museum of Art, 98

Birmingham Botanical Gardens, 58

Aldridge Gardens, 53

Red Mountain Park, 55

Ruffner Mountain, 57

Civil Rights Trail, 96

Pepper Place Market, 122

Railroad Park, 51

Moss Rock Nature Preserve, 59

CHEAP EATS

Milo's Hamburgers, 25

Barbeque, 32

Hot dogs, 24

Pizza, 26

Eagle's Soul Food, 17

Niki's West lunch, 13

Burgers at Green Valley, 23

ACTIVITIES
BY SEASON

SPRING

Wildflower garden at the Birmingham Botanical Gardens, 58

Hydrangeas at Aldridge Gardens, 53

Cahaba lilies, 48

Do Dah Day, 85

Opera Birmingham Vocal Competition, 62

Magic City Art Connection, 47

Ropes course at Red Mountain Park, 55

Baseball at Regions Field, 45

SUMMER

Sidewalk Film Festival, 81

Birmingham Zoo, 49

McWane Center, 101

Sacred Harp Singing Convention, 83

Sloss Fest, 82

Secret Stages, 88

Pepper Place, 122

Movies at Avondale Park, 52

Play golf, 42

Symphony in the Summer at Railroad Park, 51

Art on the Rocks at the Birmingham Museum of Art, 98

FALL

The views from Ruffner Mountain, 57

Haunted tours of Oak Hill Cemetery, 95

Veteran's Day parade, 84

Magic City Classic, 47

Talladega racing, 38

Gip's Place, 68

Greek Festival, 89

Moss Rock Festival, 59

Theater season, 107

Boo at the Zoo, 49

WINTER

Meet an author at Alabama Booksmith, 119

Buy Christmas Music, 120

Birmingham Ballet Nutcracker, 62

Christmas at Arlington, 94

Peavine Falls at Oak Mountain, 50

Christmas movies at the Alabama Theater, 77

Wacky Tacky Christmas Light Tour, 91